CONTENTS

Animal Absurdities

Riddles

1 **W**hat do well-behaved young lambs say to their mothers?

'Thank-ewe.'

2 **W**hat's grey and can't see well from either end?

A donkey with its eyes shut.

3 **W**hat do elephants play marbles with?

Bowling balls.

4 **W**hat asks but never answers?

An owl.

4

5 **W**hat's the same size and shape as an elephant but weighs nothing at all?

An elephant's shadow.

6 **W**hat's got six legs and can fly long distances?

Three swallows.

7 **W**hat's black and white and eats like a horse?

A zebra.

8 **W**hen is a car like a frog?

When it is being toad.

9 **H**ow do you spell 'mouse trap' with only three letters?

C A T.

10 **W**hat did the buffalo say to his son, when he went away on a long trip?

'Bison.'

11 **I**f a horse loses its tail, where can it get another one?

At a re-tail store.

12 **H**ow do you know when it's been raining cats and dogs?

You step into a poodle.

13 **H**ow many animals did Moses fit in the Ark?

None, it was Noah's Ark.

14 **H**ow do you get down from an elephant?

You don't get down from an elephant; you get down from a duck.

15 **W**hat's bright orange and sounds like a parrot?

A carrot.

16 **W**hat does an octopus wear when it's cold?

A coat of arms.

WASH DAY AT THE OCTOPUS' PLACE

17 **W**hat's the difference between a dark sky and an injured lion?

One pours with rain and the other roars with pain.

18 **W**hat would you get if you crossed a hunting dog with a journalist?

A news hound.

Ralph the Bloodhound gets his Journalism Degree, buys himself a camera and goes chasing movie stars with the paparazzi...

19 **W**hat happened to the two frogs that caught the same bug at the same time?

They were tongue-tied.

20 **I**f horses wear shoes,
what do camels wear?

Desert boots.

21 **W**hy are dolphins clever?

Because they live in schools.

22 **W**hat do bees do with
their honey?

They cell it.

HONEY
DIRECT FROM THE
MANUFACTURER

This new business
is a real buzz.

23 **W**hat do you call a cat who lives in a hospital?

A first aid kit.

24 **W**hat do you call a cat that plays football?

Puss in boots.

25 **W**hat can go as fast as a race horse?

The jockey.

26 **W**hy is the letter 't' important to a stick insect?

Because without it, it would be a sick insect.

27 **W**hy should you be careful playing against a team of big cats?

They might be cheetahs.

28 **I**'m the part of a bird that's not in the sky; I can swim in the ocean and remain dry. What am I?

Its shadow.

WOH THERE! A MINOR BIRD! I nearly stood on the little guy!

29 **W**hich bird never grows up?

The minor bird.

30 **W**hat's the difference between a bird and a fly?

A bird can fly but a fly can't bird.

31 **W**hat is more fantastic than a talking dog?

A spelling bee.

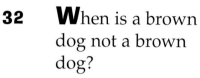

32 **W**hen is a brown dog not a brown dog?

When it's a greyhound.

33 **W**hat do you call a bee that is always complaining?

A grumble bee.

34 **H**ow do you stop a dog from digging up the front yard?

Put it out the back.

35 **W**hy does a tiger have stripes?

So it won't be spotted.

36 **W**hat is a prickly pear?

Two hedgehogs.

37 **H**ow can you tell a dogwood tree?

By its bark.

38 **W**hat do you get if you cross a worm with a baby goat?

A dirty kid.

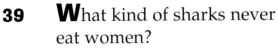

39 **W**hat kind of sharks never eat women?

Man-eating sharks!

40 **W**hat has four legs and an arm?

A happy lion.

41 **W**hy was the glowworm unhappy?

Her children weren't very bright.

42 **W**hen is it bad luck to be followed by a big black cat?

When you are a little grey mouse.

43 **W**hy are giraffes good friends to have?

Because they stick their necks out for you.

44 **W**hy was the mother flea so sad?

Because her children were going to the dogs.

45 **W**here do you find a no-legged dog?

Right where you left it.

Here, boy !!!

46 **W**hat's green and red and goes 120 km/h?

A frog in a blender.

47   **W**hat fly has laryngitis?

A horsefly (hoarse fly).

48   **W**hat's black and white and rolls down a hill?

A penguin.

49   **W**hat's black and white and laughs?

The penguin that pushed the other one.

50   **W**hat happened to the horse that swallowed a dollar?

He bucked.

51   **W**hat animal builds his house in the jungle?

A boa constructor.

52 **W**hy do gorillas have big nostrils?

Because they have big fingers.

53 **W**hat has 50 legs and can't walk?

Half a centipede.

54 **W**hat do you get when an elephant stands on your roof?

Mushed rooms.

55 **W**hat do you get if you run a sparrow over with a lawn mower?

Shredded tweet.

56 **W**hat do polar bears get from sitting on the ice too long?

Polaroids.

57 **W**hat's an army of worms called?

An apple corps.

58 **W**hat's the last thing that goes through a bug's mind as it hits a car windscreen?

His bottom.

59 **W**hat do you get when you cross a rooster with a steer?

A cock and bull story.

60 **W**hat's worse than finding a worm in your apple?

Finding half a worm!

61 **W**hat do you get if you pour hot water down a rabbit hole?

Hot cross bunnies.

62 **A** hundred feet in the air and yet my back is still on the ground. What am I?

An upside-down centipede.

63 **W**hat do you get if you sit under a cow?

A pat on the head.

64 **W**here did Noah keep the bees?

In the Ark hives.

65 **W**hich bird can lift the most?

A crane.

66 **W**hy did the lizard cross the road?

To see his flat mate.

67 **W**hat has a foot but no legs?

A snail.

68 **W**hat has four legs and flies?

A dead cat.

69 **W**hat do you call a lion wearing a hat?

A dandy lion.

70 **W**hat is grey, has a tail and a trunk but is not an elephant?

A mouse on vacation.

71 **W**hat do you call a lamb with a machine gun?

Lambo.

72 **W**hy are naughty kids like maggots?

Because they try to wiggle out of everything.

73 **W**hat do you get when you cross an automobile with a household animal?

A carpet.

74 **W**hen do you put a frog in your sister's bed?

When you can't find a mouse.

75 **W**hat are teenage giraffes told when they go on their first date?

'No necking.'

76 **W**hat grows up while growing down?

A duck.

77 **W**hy don't turkeys get invited to dinner parties?

Because they use fowl language.

HA! Did you hear the joke about the chicken crossing the road?

Oh not another one of histerrible chicken jokes!

78 **I**f a rooster laid a brown egg and a white egg, what colour would the chicks be?

Roosters don't lay eggs.

79 **W**hy wasn't the butterfly invited to the dance?

Because it was a moth ball.

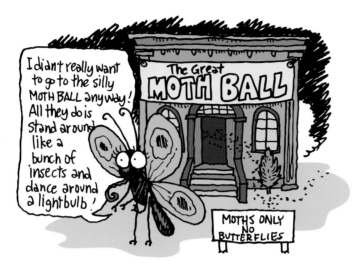

80 **I**f a man carried my burden, he'd break his back.
I am not rich, but I always leave silver in my trail.
What am I?

A snail.

81 **W**hat part of a fish weighs the most?

The scales.

82 **W**hy do
elephants
have trunks?

*Because
they can't fit
everything
in their
handbags.*

83 **W**hat do you say when you meet a toad?

'Wart's new?'

84 **W**here do you find elephants?

You don't. They're so big they don't get lost.

85 **W**hat language do birds speak?

Pigeon English.

86 **W**hat is a polygon?

A dead parrot.

I reckon I'm hot on this guy's trail!

87 **W**hat do you have when twenty rabbits step backwards?

A receding hare-line.

88 **Y**ou are in a room with a lemur, a chimpanzee and a gorilla. Which primate in the room is smartest?

You are!

89 **W**hat do you call an amorous insect?

A love bug.

90 **A** monkey, a squirrel and a bird race to the top of a coconut tree. Who reaches the banana first?

None of them. There are no bananas is coconut trees.

91 **W**hy do chickens lay eggs?

Because if they drop them they will break.

92 **W**hat walks on its head all day?

A nail in a horseshoe.

93 **W**here do fish keep their money?

In a river bank.

94 **W**ho always goes to sleep wearing shoes?

A horse.

95 **W**hat time is it when an elephant sits on your fence?

Time to get a new fence.

96 **W**ho spends all day at the window, goes to the table for meals and hides at night?

A fly.

97 **I** have a little house in which I live in all alone. It has no doors or windows, and if I want to go out I must break through the wall. What am I?

A baby bird in an egg.

98 **W**hat is the single greatest use of cowhide?

Covering cows.

99 **W**hat has four legs and can see just as well from both ends?

A horse with its eyes closed.

Tongue Twisters

100 The thick, slippery snake sneaked and slithered.

101 The fleeing fly finally flew fast.

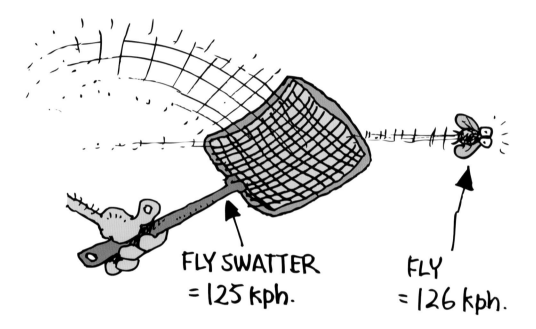

FLY SWATTER
= 125 kph.

FLY
= 126 kph.

102 Four frozen flies were free to flee.

103 The tired turtle tried to tread tenderly.

104 **T**he sleek, shiny shark swam silently.

105 **T**he drinking donkey drank delicately.

106 **O**rdinarily, ordinary orange orang utans organised orderly outings.

107 **P**olly parrot wanted wilted peppers.

108 **T**he porpoise purposely performed poetry on purpose.

109 **T**he awkward octopus awkwardly awoke.

110 **P**igeons surely shyly sit on statues.

111 **T**he dog dragged Daisy's dolly for digging.

112 **T**he stinger stung Sheryl with a sharp stab.

113 **P**aulie Bull pulled but Billy Pug bailed.

114 **W**hen Warren Rabbit really wanted he'd rush into his rabbit warren.

Gross and Gory

Riddles

115 **W**hat's invisible and smells like carrots?

Bunny farts.

116 **W**hat do you call an elephant that never washes?

A smellyphant.

117 **W**hat's yellow and smells like bananas?

Monkey vomit.

118 **H**ow can you tell when a moth farts?

It flies straight for a second.

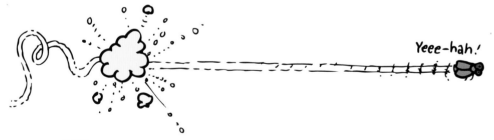

Yeee-hah!

119 **W**hat's brown and sounds like a bell?

Dung.

26

120 **W**hat do you give an elephant with diarrhoea?

Plenty of room.

When Nancy said she had a rumble in her tummy... everyone knew just what she meant!

121 **W**hat do you give a sick elephant?

A very big paper bag.

122 **W**hat's a sick joke?

Something that comes up in conversation.

123 **W**hat's the hardest part about sky diving?

The ground.

OPEN
OPEN
OPEN

124 **H**ow do you make a Venetian blind?

Poke his eyes out.

Boy! I could really go for a burger and fries!

You can get mighty hungry just laying around!

125 **H**ow can you tell if a corpse is angry?

It flips its lid.

126 **W**hat do you find up a clean nose?

Fingerprints.

127 **W**hy didn't the man die when he drank poison?

Because he was in the living room.

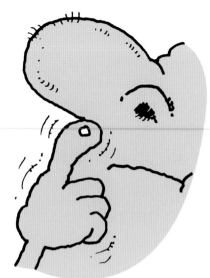

128 **W**hat's green, has two legs and sits on the end of your finger?

The boogeyman.

129 **W**hat do you do if your nose goes on strike?

Picket!

130 **W**hat do you call the red stuff between an elephant's toes?

A slow explorer.

131 **H**ow did the basketball get wet?

The players dribbled all over it.

132 **H**ow do you make a tissue dance?

Put some boogie into it.

133 **W**hat is the difference between broccoli and boogers?

Kids don't like to eat broccoli.

134 **W**hat did one toilet say to the other toilet?

'You look a bit flushed!'

135 **W**hat did the first mate see in the toilet?

The captain's log.

136 **W**hy did the surfer stop surfing?

Because the sea weed.

137 **W**hat happens when the queen burps?

She issues a royal pardon.

138 **W**hy do petrol stations always lock their toilets?

They are afraid someone might clean them.

139 **W**hy did the boy take his own toilet paper to the party?

Because he was a party pooper.

140 **W**hy do they have fences around graveyards?

Everyone is dying to get in.

141 **W**hat's green and slimy and hangs from trees?

Giraffe boogers.

142 **W**hy did the toilet paper roll down the hill?

To get to the bottom.

143 **W**hat's another name for a snail?

A booger with a crash helmet.

144 **W**hat do you do with crude oil?

Teach it some manners.

145 **H**ow do you keep flies out of the kitchen?

Put a pile of manure in the living room.

146 **W**hat's the difference between a maggot and a cockroach?

Cockroaches crunch more when you eat them.

147 **W**hat's the difference between school lunches and a pile of slugs?

School lunches are in lunch boxes.

148 **W**hat has two grey legs and two brown legs?

An elephant with diarrhoea.

149 **W**hat's yellow, brown and hairy?

Cheese on toast, dropped on carpet.

Tongue Twisters

150 **A** vampire thirstily sucked thick blood.
He glugged, gobbled, gargled and gulped.
He swished, swirled and swallowed.

151 **S**even short, slimy zombies sloshed, slipped and slid
on a shiny, slippery slide.

152 **F**our fighting farty fighters farted frequently while
fighting ferociously.

153 **O**range spew,
red spew,
yellow spew,
blue spew.

154 **P**eter Popov
popped off
presently.

155 **T**he queen quite cleverly created chaos with a steamy stinker.

156 **T**hick, slimy sticky snot.

157 **G**ooey poo on Stewie's shoe.

158 **B**rock's BO brought Bob to tears.

159 **D**oreen's double Dutch oven disgusted Darren.

160 **R**eally waxy ears are ringing.

161 **J**erry's gorbies glowed green.

162 **S**eth's stomach solemnly sent spew spewing.

163 **M**y smelly, slimy, stinky sister's sloppy nappies.

164 **S**weat-soaked smelly armpit stink.

165 **P**loppy Peter's pretty putridly pongy.

166 **F**rank's farts freaked Francine.

167 **S**ammy's sweaty shirt was soaked in sweat.
Silly Sally slipped on Sammy's sloppy sweat.
Simple Simon swam in Sammy's sweat.
Sammy simply said, 'That's wet.'

168 **T**he Blob was a blobby gooey glob.

169 **T**ongue twisters twist tongues. Twisted tongues taste terrible. Terrible tasting tongues twist tightly. A toast to tightly twisted terrible tasting tongues.

170 **S**uddenly, Samuel saw snotty Sarah stealing several strands of snot.

171 **B**ob's big burp blasted barriers.

172 **P**aul popped his pus-filled pimple.

173 **B**etty bet Poppy that pro-ballers have BO problems.

174 **G**irl gargoyle, guy gargoyle, gurgling gluey goo.

175 **E**ric's earwax was orange, obviously.

176 **G**irty gurgled good blood and bad blood.

177 **F**lora's flatulence frighteningly floored Freddy.

178 **I**f Flora farted, Francine fell and Frannie fainted, how foul was Flora's fart?

179 **C**hucky's chunder had colourful carrot chunks.

180 **O**ctavia's up-chuck was oddly orange.

181 **S**ix snot balls shot past Sally Schnell.

Game On!

Riddles

182 **W**hat is put on the table and cut, but never eaten.

A deck of cards.

183 **W**hat does every winner lose in a race?

Their breath.

184 **W**hat stories are told by basketball players?

Tall stories.

185 **W**hy did all the bowling pins go down?

They were on strike.

186 **W**hat has 22 legs and two wings but cannot fly?

A soccer team.

187 **W**hich goalkeeper can jump higher than a crossbar?

All of them – a crossbar can't jump!

188 **W**hy did the footballer take a piece of rope onto the pitch?

He was the skipper.

189 **W**hat part of a football ground smells the best?

The scenter spot.

190 **W**hen are babies like basketball players?

When they dribble.

Game On!

191 **W**hat do you call a cat that plays football?

Puss in boots.

192 **W**hat illness do martial artists get?

Kung flu.

193 **W**hy were the arrows nervous?

Because they were all in a quiver.

194 **W**ho was the fastest runner in the whole world?

Adam, because he was the first in the human race.

195 **W**hat race is never run?

A swimming race.

196 **W**hat did one bowling ball say to the other?

'Don't stop me, I'm on a roll!'

39

197 **W**hat's the best way to win a race?

Run faster than everyone else.

198 **W**here do old bowling balls end up?

In the gutter.

This sort of gutter is no place for an old bowling ball!

199 **W**hat was the fly doing in the lady's soup?

Backstroke.

200 **W**hy was the boxer known as Picasso?

Because he spent all his time on the canvas.

201 **W**hy don't grasshoppers go to football matches?

They prefer cricket matches.

202 **W**hat is the smelliest sport?

Ping pong!

Forget the cricket or football matches ...I'd rather just sit around chewing a leaf

203 **W**hy aren't football stadiums built in outer space?

Because there is no atmosphere!

204 **W**hy is tennis such a noisy game?

Because everyone raises a racket.

205 **W**hy did the bicycle keep falling over?

Because it was two tired.

206 **W**hen is it handy to have toes?

When you go to a foot ball.

207 **W**hat is harder to catch the faster you run?

Your breath.

Tongue Twisters

208 **W**ayne likes white-water rafting after work.

There's not even a river around here!

BUS STOP

Tired of catching the bus, Wayne decides to white-water raft his way home.

209 **B**ree's billiards brilliance bewildered Brooke.

210 **A** broad bloke boxed blindly.

211 **T**revor's trophy for table tennis triumph was terrific.

212 **B**oris beat Barney in breaststroke.

213 **R**ight hook, left hook, uppercut, left jab.

214 **S**printing Sally hurdled hurdles.

215 **A**thletic athletes are, at least, athletically athletic.

216 **T**he athletes decided to discuss discus delegations.

217 **S**hot-puts squash feet.

218 **C**allum's karate class created classic karate kicks.

219 **T**he fighters frightened fans fighting a frighteningly fearsome fight.

220 **T**he wild, wide wrestler went whacko.

221 **T**he quick quiet cricketer requested cricketing competition.

222 **S**tanley loved sitting, sipping soda on his sofa, seeing stunned skiers stacking in snow. Seriously, Stanley loved seeing sporting slip-ups.

223 **P**rince Paul played polo pretty poorly.

224 **W**restlers wearing lycra are really weird.

225 **T**he good golfer's green golf glove.

226 **R**elay runners run relays really regularly.

227 **P**aul played plinky, plonky ping-pong.

228 **B**arbara's barbed-wire barbell.

229 **F**loundering Freya felt the burn.

230 **D**arren dropped a dumbbell on his dad.

231 **S**andy skipped swiftly.

232 **B**iceps, triceps, thigh sets, high reps.

233 **S**andy surely showed super cycling style.

234 Tim took training tips and the training tips Tim took taught Tim to train.

235 Tony tried Terry's treadmill.

236 The golfer gripped the golf grip grudgingly.

237 Sarah's sixth cycling session surely sucked.

238 Bobby the baseballer briefly broke baseball bats by bashing baseballs.

239 Push-ups, press-ups, pull-ups, sit-ups.

240   Peggy Babcock puffed and panted in pump class.

241   Skeeter's skiing school skied slowly.

242   Brad's bulging biceps burst.

243   Stewart slipped and tripped on the steep slope he trekked.

244   Brandon's black boxing gloves broke bashing punching bags.

The Five Senses

Riddles

245 What can you hear but not see and only speaks when it is spoken to?

An echo.

246 What has eyes that cannot see, a tongue that cannot taste and a soul that cannot die?

A shoe.

247 What is there more of the less you see?

Darkness.

248 What can you hold without touching?

Your breath.

249 **W**hy did the Invisible Man's wife understand him so well?

Because she could see right through him.

250 **W**hat can you hold but never touch?

A conversation.

251 **W**hat kind of music do fathers like to sing?

Pop music.

252 **W**hat did the parents say to their son who wanted to play drums?

'Beat it!'

253 **W**hat did one ear say to the other ear?

'Between you and me, we need a haircut.'

254 **W**hat can be caught but never seen?

A remark.

525

5

255 **W**hat did the ear 'ear?

Only the nose knows.

256 **W**hat tastes better than it smells?

A tongue.

257 **Y**ou can touch me, but not see me. You can throw me out, but not away. What am I?

Your back.

258 **W**hy should you never tell secrets in a grocery store?

Because the corn has ears, potatoes have eyes and beanstalk.

259 **W**hy do farts smell?

So that deaf people can appreciate them too.

260 **W**hat did the floor say to the desk?

I can see your drawers.

261 **W**hat do you think when you see a monster?

I hope he hasn't seen me.

262 **T**he person who makes it doesn't need it, the person who buys it doesn't use it and the person who uses it can't see or hear it. What is it?

A coffin.

263 **W**hat kind of music do zombies like best?

Soul.

264 **W**hat did the digital clock say to its mother?

Look Mum, no hands!

265 **W**hat smells funny?

Clown poo.

266 **W**ho is the smelliest person in the world?

King Pong.

267 **W**hat has eyes but cannot see?

A potato.

268 **S**ay my name and I disappear. What am I?

Silence.

269 **W**hat's the difference between an oral thermometer and a rectal thermometer?

The taste.

Tongue Twisters

270 **F**ergus felt furry fungus.

271 **L**arry liked licking yellow lollies.

272 **H**igh notes, low notes, fast notes, slow notes, loud notes, soft notes, big nose, no nose.

273 **T**revor's triangle tinkled and tingled.

274 **S**eth's breath smelled like death.

275 **W**hich wise guy's eyes spied the high-priced prize?

276 **T**he selfish elf ate shellfish.

277 **T**en top-notch cops felt fob watch knobs.

278 **T**he deer's ears clearly hear another deer's fairly near.

279 **F**reddy's feet smelled foul.

280 **T**he brilliant big brass band played beautifully.

281 **S**heila said she smelled Schmidt shaving.

282 **T**erry tastes twelve turnips, turning Terry's tongue numb.

283 **Y**ola loves yummy gumbo.

284 **S**imon sang several sweet-sounding songs.

285 A small, steamy smell silently slipped out.

286 Chase chews cod. Cows chew cod. If cows chase Chase, is a Chase a cod-chewing cow?

287 The crazy composer caused chaos, creating cringe-worthy compositions.

288 Can the toucan touch two tin cans?

289 Morose music makes Margaret mournful.

290 **K**im counted colours she could see on Shaun's couch.

291 **B**rad's bassoon broke, bruising Brad badly.

292 **T**he drummer dumbly decided to drum at dawn.

293 **H**orace hid when he heard Herod honking.

294 **V**iolent violinist.

295 The string section suddenly went on strike, sending shockwaves shooting through the symphony.

296 After the opera, Owen often opted for orange juice.

297 Stacey baked stinky scones.

298 Muriel miraculously made magical music. Actually, Muriel's miraculously magical music was marvellous.

299 Trevor terribly trumpeted till Trixie trampled Trevor's trumpet.

Crazy Critters & Cool Characters

Riddles

300 **W**hat would you call Superman if he lost all his powers?

Man.

301 **W**hat did one angel say to the other angel?

'Halo.'

302 **W**ho is scared of wolves and swears?

Little Rude Riding Hood.

303 **W**here do you find giant snails?

At the ends of their fingers.

304 **H**ow did the Vikings send messages?

By Norse code.

305 **W**hat is big, red and eats rocks?

A big, red rock eater.

306 **W**hich of the witch's friends eats the fastest?

The goblin.

307 **W**hat's the closest thing to silver?

The Lone Ranger's bottom.

308 **W**hat is Dracula's favourite fruit?

Necktarines.

309 **W**hat do Alexander the Great and Kermit the Frog have in common?

The same middle name!

310 **W**hy was Thomas Edison able to invent the light bulb?

Because he was very bright.

Hope this stops me coffin

COFFIN MIXTURE

311 **W**hy did Dracula take medicine?

To stop his coffin.

312 **W**hy did the vampire go to the orthodontist?

To improve his bite.

313 **W**hat's the difference between Santa Claus and a warm dog?

Santa wears the suit, but the dog just pants.

314 **W**hy did Henry VIII have so many wives?

He liked to chop and change.

315 **W**ho steals from her Grandma's house?

Little Red Robbin Hood.

316 **W**hy is the vampire so unpopular?

Because he is a pain in the neck.

317 **W**hat kind of cheese do monsters eat?

Monsterella!

318 **D**uring which battle was Lord Nelson killed?

His last one.

319 **W**hat did Cinderella say when her photos didn't arrive?

'Some day my prints will come.'

320 **W**ho delivers Christmas present to the wrong houses?

Santa Flaws.

321 **W**hat do monsters have mid-morning?

A coffin break.

322 **W**hat did Santa Claus's wife say during the thunderstorm?

'Come and look at the rain, dear.'

323 **W**hat job does Dracula have with the Transylvanian baseball team?

He's the bat boy.

Now when you get out there... I want to see HOME RUNS from you guys!

324 **W**ho was the father of the Black Prince?

Old King Coal.

325 **H**ow did Noah steer the Ark at night?

He switched on the floodlights.

326 **W**hy did the young vampire follow his dad's profession?

Because it was in his blood.

Dad, what should I be when I grow up?

Well let's just say... With those teeth my boy... you won't be a crane driver.

327 **W**hat's the name of a clever monster?

Frank Einstein.

328 **W**hich bus could sail the oceans?

Columbus.

329 **W**hat did the cannibal say to the explorer?

'Nice to eat you.'

330 **W**hat do you get if you cross a skunk with a bear?

Winnie the Pooh.

331 **W**hat does a monster call his parents?

Dead and Mummy.

332 **W**hy do witches get good bargains?

They're good at haggling.

333 **W**hy did the Cyclops give up teaching?

Because he only had one pupil.

334 **W**hy don't cannibals eat comedians?

Because they taste funny.

335 **W**hat feature do witches love on their computers?

The spell-checker.

336 **W**hat do you call a witch that lives at the beach?

A sand witch!

337 **W**hat does a ghost read every day?

His horrorscope.

338 **W**hat did King Kong say when his sister had a baby?

'Well, I'll be a monkey's uncle!'

339 **W**here does Dracula wash?

In a bloodbath.

340 **W**hat do vampires cross the sea in?

Blood vessels.

341 **W**hy did the zombie decide to stay in his coffin?

He felt rotten.

342 **W**hen do ghosts usually appear?

Just before someone screams.

343 **W**here does Dracula go fishing?

In a bloodstream.

344 **W**hat did the witch say to the vampire?

'Get a life!'

345 **W**hat do you get when you cross a computer with a vampire?

Love at first byte.

346 **H**ow do monsters like their eggs?

Terrifried.

347 **S**now White and the Seven Dwarfs were having dinner. The dwarfs asked for more food so Snow White got them some. How many seconds did she take?

Seven.

348 **W**hat does a monster eat after he's been to the dentist?

The dentist.

349 **W**hat do sea monsters eat?

Fish and ships.

350 **W**hat do you do with a blue monster?

Try to cheer him up a bit.

351 **W**ho is the best dancer at a monster party?

The boogie man.

352 **W**hat should you take if a monster invites you to dinner?

Someone who can't run as fast as you.

353 **W**hy isn't the Abominable Snowman scared of people?

Because he doesn't believe in them.

354 **W**hat does a monster mummy say to her kids at dinnertime?

'Don't chew with someone in your mouth.'

355 **W**hy did the monster eat his music teacher?

Because his Bach was worse than his bite.

356 **W**hat's a witch's favourite school subject?

Spelling.

357 **O**n which day do monsters eat people?

Chewsday.

358 **W**hat do ghosts use to type letters?

A type-frighter.

359 **W**hy are Cyclops couples happy together?

Because they always see eye to eye.

360 **W**hat does a boy monster do when a girl monster rolls her eyes at him?

He rolls them back to her.

361 **W**hy do ghosts hate rain?

It dampens their spirits.

362 **W**hat do you call a good-looking, kind and considerate monster?

A complete failure.

363 **W**hy don't ghosts bother telling lies?

Because you can see right through them.

364 **W**hat do you call the winner of a monster beauty contest?

Ugly.

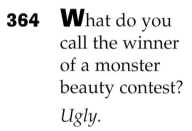

365 **W**hat type of horses do monsters ride?

Night mares.

366 **W**hat do you call a fairy that hasn't taken a bath?

Stinkerbell.

367 **W**hat weapon was most feared by medieval knights?

A can opener.

368 **H**ow does a yeti feel when it gets a cold?

Abominable.

369 **W**hat's green, sits in the corner and cries?

The Incredible Sulk.

370 **I**f you crossed the Loch Ness monster with a shark, what would you get?

Loch jaws.

371 **W**hat did the skeleton say to the twin witches?

Which witch is which?

372 **H**ow many witches does it take to change a light bulb?

Just one, but she changes it into a toad.

373 **W**here do skeletons go swimming?

In the dead sea.

374 **W**hat game do young ghosts love?

Hide and shriek.

375 **H**ow can you tell what a ghost is getting for its birthday?

By feeling its presents.

376 **W**hat illness does a ghost get from eating Christmas decorations?

Tinselitis.

377 **W**hat should you say when you meet a ghost?

'How do you boo, sir?'

378 **W**hat does a vampire never order at a restaurant?

Stake.

That's exactly why I never order steak. They always get the order wrong.

379 **W**hy didn't the skeleton go to the dance?

He had no body to go with.

380 **H**ow do you make a skeleton laugh?

Tickle his funnybone.

381 **D**o zombies have trouble getting dates?

No, they can usually dig someone up.

Tongue Twisters

382 **M**allory the mermaid mostly made mischief.

383 **A** pixie presently picked a perfect present.

384 **M**ermaids mainly mingle in lagoons.

385 **C**lara cleverly created classic car tricks.

386 **T**he greedy giant ground bones.

387 **G**rant the giant generally jogged gratefully.

When Grant jogged, the Earth shook.

388 **T**he gabbling, gargling goblin gobbled and gargled.

389 **T**he braggin', arrogant, boastin' dragon.

390 **B**read grinding bones.

391 **S**lick Trixie, the tricky pixie, picked sticks.

392 **A** werewolf was really wary of rabies.

393 Michael's mighty mystical magic manipulated Maxine.

394 Casting and conjuring and creating confusion, illuminating and inventing and instigating illusion.

395 Trudy tried teaching Tyler trickery.

396 Wally wished he was a wizard. Why did Wally wish for wizardry? Really, what Wally wanted was really wicked wizard wear.

397 Which wicked witch was wickedly wicked?

398 **F**ive fairies flipped five flapjacks.

399 **A** whacky wizard with white whiskers waved his wand.

400 **T**he wry wizard regularly worked on wand waving.

401 **T**he sorcerer practised prickly imprisoning potions privately; practising privately perfected potions perfectly.

402 **T**he alien alliance allowed acrobat eating.

403 **T**he grinning gargoyle greedily gobbled green grapes.

404 Horrid Harriet hated Halloween.
Horrid Harriet found Halloween harrowing.
Horrid Harriet had had it with Halloween,
So Horrid Harriet holidayed in Hawaii.

405 Frankenstein found France frustrating.

406 Ghastly ghosts and grinning ghouls.

407 A werewolf's whiskers rarely waver.

408 Good ghosts generally greet guests jovially.

409 Which witch doctor rain danced?

Perfectly Prehistoric

Riddles

410 **W**hat do you get when a dinosaur skydives?

A big hole.

411 **W**hy are old dinosaur bones kept in a museum?

Because they can't find any new ones.

412 **W**hat do you get if you cross a dinosaur with a vampire?

A blood shortage.

I vant to sark your blurd...

413 **H**ow do dinosaurs pass exams?

With extinction.

414 **W**hat do you get if you give a dinosaur a pogo stick?

Big holes in your driveway.

415 **W**hat do you call a dinosaur that destroys everything in its path?

Tyrannosaurus Wrecks.

416 **W**hat do you call a dinosaur that's a noisy sleeper?

Brontosnorus.

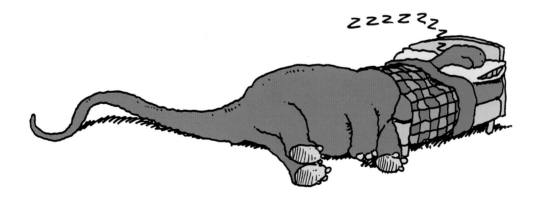

417 **W**hat do you call a blind dinosaur?

Do-ya-think-he-saurus.

418 **W**hat does a Triceratops sit on?

Its Tricera-bottom!

419 **W**hat's worse than
a Tyrannosaurus
with a toothache?

*A Diplodocus with a
sore throat.*

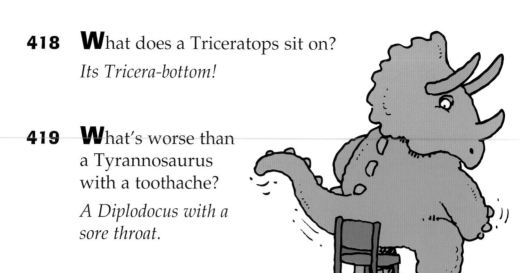

420 **W**hat do you get if
you cross a dinosaur with a dog?

A very nervous postman.

421 **W**hy don't more dinosaurs join the police force?

They can't hide behind billboards.

422 **W**hat did the egg say to the dinosaur?

'You're egg-stinct.'

423 **W**hy didn't the dinosaur cross the road?

Because roads weren't invented.

424 **W**hy couldn't the long-necked dinosaur see?

Because his head was in the clouds.

425 **W**hat do you call a group of people who dig for dinosaur bones?

A skeleton crew.

426 **W**hat do you call a scared Tyrannosaurus?

A nervous rex.

427 **W**hat's extinct and works in rodeos?

Broncosaurus.

428 **W**hat do you call a dinosaur eating a taco?
Tyrannosaurus Mex.

429 **W**hen did the last dinosaur die?
After the second-last dinosaur.

430 **W**hat do you call a 100-million-year-old dinosaur?
A fossil.

431 **W**hat do dinosaurs put on their floors?
Rep-tiles.

432 **W**hat's the hardest part of making dinosaur stew?
Finding a pot big enough to hold the dinosaur.

433 **W**hy did the baby dinosaur get arrested?

Because he took the bus home.

434 **W**hat has a spiked tail, plates on its back and 16 wheels?

A Stegosaurus on roller skates.

Tongue Twisters

435 **A** brachiosaurus bellowed with bronchitis.

436 **B**ronwyn bathed the baby brontosaurus in blue bathwater.

437 **T**he fabulous fabrosaurus fabricated fabulously.

438 **T**wo tricky trilobites tickled Trixie.

439 The terribly tiring Pterydactyl was tragically trapped.

440 Saltasaurus shins should be shaved and saved.

441 The dopey dinosaur drank and dived and drowned.

442 Warren wanted a real wheel to do real wheelies;
What Warren really wanted was a real wheel.
Warren wished wheels were real,
But for cavemen wheels weren't real.

443 The saber-tooth slayed a sleuth.

444 **T**he creepy caveman crept quite creepily.

445 **T**he spiky stegosaurus sipped a soda.

446 **T**he tricky triceratops tripped a tyrannosaurus.

447 **T**he brown brontosaurus borrowed bright but bland books.

448 **M**anny was a whale while Sammy was a mammoth.

449 **N**aughty Neanderthals neatly gnawed a nifty numbat.

450 The itchy Iguanodon insists on eating Iggy's insects.

451 Fred found freaky fossils that fuelled his fire for finding facts.

452 The bootblack brought the Brachiosaur's black boot back.

453 Sneaky sauropods eat selfish shellfish.

454 Shy Styracosaurus sometimes sheds a single shiny tear.

455 **V**era the vivacious Velociraptor visits Vic with vigour.

456 **A**n affable Afrovenator aptly ate an apple after every act.

457 **C**an Camarasaurus catch a crafty Camaro?

458 **S**ixty-seven thick, thoughtless, sick stegosauruses stuck spikes in twenty-two trapped tyrannosauruses.

459 **S**tewie the stegosaurus slept soundly; Stewie the stegosaurus snored solidly.

Tough and Tricky

Riddles

460 **W**hat's easier to give than receive?
Criticism.

461 **W**hat kind of dress can never be worn?
Your address.

462 **W**hat's the last thing you take off before bed?
Your feet off the floor.

463 **W**hat can go up a chimney down, but not down a chimney up?
An umbrella.

464 **W**hat starts working only when it's fired?

A rocket.

465 **W**hat is always coming but never arrives?

Tomorrow.

466 **W**hat stays in the corner but travels all around the world?

A postage stamp.

467 **W**hat do you put in a barrel to make it lighter?

A hole.

468 **W**hat comes down but never goes up?

Rain.

469 **W**hat gets wet the more you dry?

A towel.

470 **W**hat sort of ring is always square?

A boxing ring.

471 **W**hat kind of bow can't be tied?

A rainbow.

472 **W**hat runs all around a pasture but never moves?

A fence.

473 **I** am tall when I'm young and short when I'm old, what am I?

A candle.

474 **W**hat goes up and down but never moves?

A flight of stairs.

475 **W**hich candle burns longer, a red one or a green one?

Neither. They both burn shorter.

476 **W**hat belongs to you but is used more by other people?

Your name.

477 **W**hat's always taken before you get it?

Your picture.

478 **P**oor people have me.
Rich people need me.
If you eat me you die.
What am I?

Nothing.

479 **W**hat can you give away but also keep?

A cold.

480 **W**hat can run but can't walk?

A river.

481 **B**etty rode into town on Friday, and rode out again two days later, on Friday. How?

Friday was the horse's name.

482 **I**f a yellow house is made of yellow bricks and a red house is made of red bricks, what is a green house made of?

Glass.

483 **W**hat goes up and does not come down?

Your age.

484 **I** only point in one direction, but I guide people around the world. What am I?

A compass.

485 **W**hat has a head and a tail but no legs?

A coin.

486 **W**hat do you call someone who doesn't have all their fingers on one hand?

Normal. You have fingers on both hands.

487 **W**hat was the highest mountain in the world before Mt Everest was discovered?

Mt Everest.

488 **W**hat is higher without the head than with it?

A pillow.

489 Take off my skin and I won't cry, but you will. What am I?

An onion.

490 What can you draw without a pencil or paper?

The blinds.

491 What runs down the street but has no legs?

The kerb.

492 What has holes but still holds water?

A sponge.

493 What goes up when rain comes down?

An umbrella.

494 **W**hat flies all day but
never goes anywhere?

A flag.

495 **W**hat goes around the
house and in the house but
never touches the house?

The sun.

496 **T**he more of these you take, the more you leave
behind.

Footsteps.

497 **W**hat is brown when you buy it, red when you use
it, and black when you throw it away?

Firewood.

498 **E**veryone has one and they can't lose it. What is it?

A shadow.

ARRRHH!
That thing's been
following me
ever since the
sun came up,
this morning!

499 **W**hat has many rings but no fingers?

A telephone.

500 **W**hat has two legs but can't walk?

A pair of pants.

501 **W**hat US state is round on both sides and high in the middle?

Ohio.

502 **W**hat kind of ship never sinks?

Friendship.

503 **W**hy did the bungee jumper take a vacation?

Because he was at the end of his rope.

504 **W**hy are good intentions like people who faint?

They both need carrying out.

505 **W**hat is always running but never gets anywhere?

A refrigerator.

506 **W**hen is a door not a door?

When it is ajar.

507 **W**hat's a liquid that won't freeze?

Hot water.

508 **W**hat has two hands, no fingers, stands still and goes?

A clock.

509 **W**hat gets bigger and bigger the more you take away from it?

A hole.

510 **H**ow can a pocket be empty but still have something in it?

It can have a hole in it.

511 **I**n a one-storey pink house with pink windows, pink walls, pink doors and pink floors lived a girl with a pink cat which even had pink paws. What colour were the stairs?

There were no stairs. It was a one-storey house.

512 **A** dad and his son had an accident and were taken to different hospitals. Upon seeing the boy, his surgeon said, 'I can't operate on you. You're my son.' How is that possible?

The surgeon was the boy's mother.

513 **W**hat has no legs but is always walking?

A pair of shoes.

514 **I** can breathe and I will eat what you feed me, but if you give me water I will die. What am I?

A fire.

515 **Y**ou are lost in a cold dark cave. You have a match, a kerosene lamp and a candle. Which do you light first?

The match.

516 **A** man was driving his truck without his lights on and the moon was not out, yet he still managed to spot a rabbit run out on the road. How?

It was daylight.

517 **I**f an electric train is travelling south and the wind is blowing north, in which direction would the smoke travel?

There is no smoke from an electric train.

518 **W**hat has an eye but cannot see?

A needle.

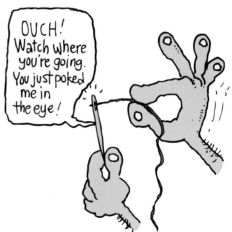

519 **W**hat is the only certain way you can double your money?

Look at it in the mirror.

520 **S**unday, Tim and Tom had lunch and one of them paid the bill. It wasn't Tim or Tom, so who was it?

Their friend Sunday.

521 **W**hat has a bed but never sleeps, can run but never walks and a bank but no money?

A river.

522 **W**hat loses its head in the morning but gets it back at night?

A pillow.

523 **W**hat has teeth but cannot eat?

A comb.

524 **W**hat sort of person stands around making faces all day?

A watchmaker.

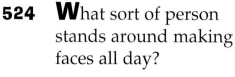

525 **I** have keys but no locks. I have space but no room. You can enter but not go inside. What am I?

A keyboard.

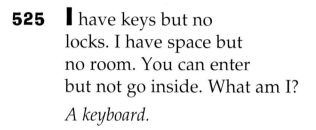

526 **W**hat goes around and around the wood but never goes into the wood?

The bark of a tree.

527 **I** always tell the truth and I copy everything I see. What am I?

A mirror.

528 **W**here do you find roads without cars, forests without trees and towns without houses?

On a map!

529 **W**hat question can you never honestly answer yes to?

Are you asleep?

530 **W**ho is your mother's brother's brother-in-law?

Your dad.

531 **W**hy can't someone living to the north of a river be buried to the south of the river?

Because they are still alive.

532 **W**hat is better than the best thing and worse than the worst thing?

Nothing.

533 **W**hat has no beginning, end or middle?

A doughnut.

534 **W**hat grows up while growing down?
A duckling.

535 **W**hat do you throw out when you need to use it, and take it back when you don't need it anymore?
An anchor.

536 **F**orward I am heavy, backward I am not. What am I?
A ton.

537 **I** am lighter than air but even a million men couldn't lift me up. What am I?
A bubble.

538 **W**hat runs across the floor without legs?
Water.

539 **W**hat stays where it is even after it goes off?

An alarm clock.

540 **I** have an eye but cannot see, and am strong and fast but have no limbs. What am I?

A hurricane.

541 **A** box without hinges, lock or key, but a golden treasure lies in me. What am I?

An egg.

542 **I**t's been around for thousands of years but is never more than a month old. What is it?

The moon.

543 **W**hat kind of coat can you put on only when it's wet?

A coat of paint.

544 **W**hat weighs more, a kilo of lead or a kilo of feathers?

They both weigh the same.

545 **B**rothers and sisters I have none, but that man's father is my father's son. Who is that man?

My son.

546 **I**f you have me you want to share me, but if you share me you haven't got me. What am I?

A secret.

547 **W**hat creature walks on four legs when young, two legs when it grows up and three legs when it's old?

A person. Babies crawl, adults walk and elderly people use a cane.

548 **T**here is a green house that contains a white house that contains a pink house which contains lots of babies. What is it?

A watermelon.

549 I am mined and then shut up in a wooden case from which I am never released, and yet I am used by lots of people. What am I?

A pencil lead.

550 What is something you can keep after giving it to someone else?

Your word.

551 When I do it up it walks but when I loosen it, it stops.

A sandal.

552 You can draw me, shoot me and load me but I'm made of nothing. What am I?

A blank.

553 There are many different types but the one you pick doesn't do its job. What is it?

A lock.

554   **W**hat is bought in yards and worn by feet?

Carpet.

555   **I**'m measured in temperature (degrees) and time (minutes and seconds), but have neither. What am I?

Longitude and latitude.

556   **I**f a woman is born in China, grows up in Australia, lives in America and dies in London, what is she?

Dead.

557   **A** king, queen, and two twins all lay in a large room. How are there no adults in the room?

They are all beds.

Tongue Twisters

558 Toy boat (this one looks easy, but say it ten times fast!).

559 Polly peddled Polish sausage.

560 Huge imps sink ships, pink chimps use shrinks.

561 Theoretically, the thirteenth shopfront shouldn't shut.

562 Neal nearly kneeled nearby.

563   **H**arry hurriedly hopped happily.

564   **A** big bug bit a bold bald bear.

565   **L**eft leg, right leg, red leg, yellow leg.

566   **T**he poet poetically promised prime political poetry.

567   **W**endy whispered, Yanni yelled, Ryan roared.
Wendy whispered, Yanni yelled, Ryan roared.
Wendy roared, Yanni whispered, Ryan yelled.
Wendy, Yanni, Ryan yelled, whispered roared.

568 Sloppy Salina's slippers sadly slipped, sending Salena sliding and slipping.

569 Mak met Mike; Mike met Mak;
Mike and Mak met Matt;
Mike, Mak and Matt met Mark;
Mike, Mak, Matt and Mark met Bob.

570 Frieda's frantically funny face froze when the westerly wind wafted.

571 Wiley Wilma Wilmington was wilfully wilfull.

572 In general, in January, Jenny generally generalised.

573 The freezing freezer froze fast.
The fast freezing freezer feels frozen.
The frozen freezer finally defrosted.

574 Barry brought
brilliant butter.

575 Troy Boy
bought Joy soy
with joy.

576 Black background,
brown background,
blue background.

577 Six thick thistles stick.

578 **S**ally's sore sore sure was sore.

579 **W**ally wasn't really whimsical;
Wally wandered what whimsical was.
Witty was what Wally wanted,
And witty was what Wally resoundingly was.

580 **A**n imaginary menagerie manager imagined
managing many menageries.

581 **R**ed lorries,
yellow lollies.

582 **W**ally wore an
Irish wristwatch.
When wound,
Wally's Irish
wristwatch
worked well.

583 'Sure, Samantha,' shy Shelley said shyly.
She certainly shook and seemed to shimmy.
Samantha smiled and served shanks.
'Thanks,' said Shelley.

584 Which witch wished which wicked wish?

585 Unique New York.

586 Six sharp smart sharks.

Five smart sharks   One not-so-bright shark.

587 **S**he sifted thistles through her thistle sifter.

588 **A** box of biscuits, a batch of mixed biscuits.

589 **P**eter Piper picked a peck of pickled peppers. If Peter Piper picked a peck of pickled peppers, where's the peck of pickled peppers Peter Piper picked?

Now that's a hot pickle!

590 **S**he sells seashells by the seashore. The sea shells that she sells are seashore shells I'm sure.

100% GUARANTEED SEASHORE SHELLS

SALE

591 **R**ubber baby buggy bumpers.

592 **R**ound the rugged rocks the ragged rascal ran.

593 **A** boy stoat stole Troy's toy boat.

594 **A**re our oars oak?

595 **F**red fed Ned bread; Ned fed Fred bread.

596 **G**irl apes gripe about Greek grapes.

597 **S**hould Stu choose the shoes he chews?

598 **I** slit the sheet and on the slitted sheet I sit.

599 **I**s this your sister's sixth zither, Mister?

600 **A** laurel-crowned clown.

601 **T**he local yokel yodels.

602 **M**any an anemone sees an enemy anemone.

Letters and Numbers

Riddles

603 **W**hat word is always spelled incorrectly?
Incorrectly.

604 **W**hat starts with a 'P', ends with an 'E', and has a million letters in it?
Post Office.

605 **W**hat ten-letter word starts with fuel?
Automobile.

606 **W**hat is the beginning of eternity, the end of time, and the beginning of every ending?
The letter 'E'.

607 **W**hen Adam introduced himself to Eve, which three words did he use that read the same backward and forward?

'Madam, I'm Adam.'

608 **T**wo fathers and their sons go fishing. Each catches a fish, which is three in total. How is that possible?

The fishermen are a grandfather, father and son.

609 **H**ow many 2-cent stamps are in a dozen?

12. There are 12 of anything in a dozen.

610 **W**hat starts with an 'E', ends with an 'E', and only has one letter in it?

Envelope.

611 **W**hat word if pronounced right is wrong and if pronounced wrong is right?

Wrong.

612 **W**hat has four
fingers and a thumb
but is not a hand?

A glove.

613 **W**hich letter of the
alphabet holds the
most water?

The 'C'.

614 **W**here does Friday come before Wednesday?

In the dictionary.

615 **W**hat's the centre of gravity?

The letter 'V'.

All of this tumbling around in zero gravity is making me giddy.

I'll be glad to get back in the space ship.

616 **W**hich months have 28 days?

All of them.

617 **W**hat's the letter that ends everything?

The letter 'G'.

618 **N**ame three inventions that have helped man up in the world.

The elevator, the ladder and the alarm clock.

619 **W**hy is the Mississippi such an unusual river?

It has four 'I's and can't even see.

620 **H**ow many seconds are there in a year?

Twelve: 2nd of January, 2nd of February…

621 **W**hen does 'B' come after 'U'?

When you take some of its honey.

622 **W**hat's green, has eight legs and would kill you if it fell on you from out of a tree?

A billiard table.

623 **W**hat is the longest word in the world?

Smiles, because there is a mile between the beginning and the end.

624 **I** have ten legs, 20 arms and 54 feet. What am I?

A liar.

625 **W**hy can't a nose be more than 11 inches long?

If it was any longer it would be a foot.

626 **I**f Jill has 1.5 sand piles and Jesse has 2.5 sand piles and you combine them, how many sand piles would there be?

One.

627 **H**ow do you get four suits for a couple of dollars?

Buy a deck of cards.

628 **T**hree men were in a boat. It capsized but only two got their hair wet. Why?

The third man was bald.

629 **W**hat has a hundred legs but can't walk?

Fifty pairs of pants.

630 **W**hat's the hottest letter in the alphabet?

It's 'B', because it makes oil boil.

631 **W**hy was the maths book sad?

Because it had so many problems.

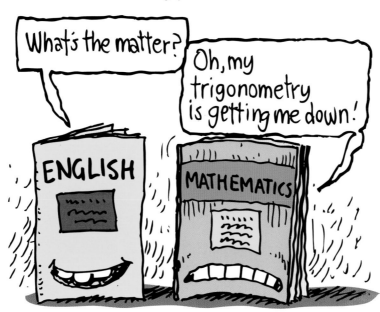

632 **W**hen do mathematicians die?

When their number is up.

633 **W**hat puzzles make you angry?

Crossword puzzles.

634 **W**hen does the alphabet only have 24 letters?

When 'U' and 'I' aren't there.

635 **W**hy was the baby pen crying?

Because its mum was doing a long sentence.

636 **I** make up all literature, but I'm often sealed. What am I?

Letters.

637 **H**ow do you make seven an even number?

Take off the 'S'.

638 **W**hich animals are best at maths?

Rabbits, because they're always multiplying.

639 **W**hat word becomes shorter when you add two letters to it?

Short.

640 **W**hat occurs once in a minute, twice in a moment and never in a thousand years?

The letter 'M'.

641 **W**hat starts with 'T', ends with 'T' and has 'T' in it?

A teapot.

642 **H**ow do you make the number 'one' disappear?

Add a 'g' and it's 'gone'.

643 **I**f two's company and three's a crowd, what are four and five?

Nine.

644 **W**hat has 88 keys but can't open a single door?

A piano.

645 **W**hat do the numbers 11, 69 and 88 have in common?

They all read the same upside-down.

646 **W**hen things go wrong, what can you always count on?

Your fingers.

647 If you took two apples from three apples, how many would you have?

The two you took.

648 What is at the end of the world?

The letter 'D'.

649 What did the zero say to the eight?

'I like your belt!'

650 How did the soccer fan know before the game that the score would be 0-0?

The score is always 0-0 before the game.

651 What has four legs but cannot walk?

A table.

652 **W**hy did the cat sit on the computer?

To keep an eye on the mouse.

653 **F**red has five daughters and each daughter has one brother. How many siblings are there?

Six. All five daughters have the same one brother.

654 **W**hat did the robber get when he stole a calendar?

12 months.

655 **H**ow many apples can you put in an empty box?

One. After that it's not empty anymore.

656 **W**hat bet can never be won?

The alphabet.

657 **W**hat has a hundred limbs but cannot walk?

A tree.

658 **W**hat is bigger when it's upside down?

The number 6.

659 **I**f I have it, I don't share it. If I share it, I don't have it. What is it?

A secret.

660 **W**hat was even more useful than the invention of the first telephone?

The second telephone.

661 **W**hy was number ten scared?

Because seven ate nine.

662 **W**hat is a forum?

One-um plus three-um.

663 **W**hat word is always spelled wrong?

Wrong.

664 **H**ow do you know when a spider is popular?

When it has its own website.

665 **Y**ou have a barrel of water and you need exactly one litre of water from it. How can you figure out one litre if you only have a 3L and a 5L container?

Fill the 3L container and pour into the 5L container. Fill the 3L again and fill the 5L from it. There will be one litre left in the 3L container.

666 **T**he doctor gives you three tablets and tells you to take one every half hour. How long before you run out of tablets?

One hour. You take them at 0 mins, 30 mins and 1 hr.

667 **H**ow can "L" be greater in size than "XL"?

Roman numerals.

668 **H**ow do you share 32 apples evenly with 34 people?

Make apple sauce.

669 **W**hat do you call a man who shaves 15 times a day?

A barber.

Tongue Twisters

670   **O**ne smart man felt smart. Two smart men felt smart. Three smart men felt smart. They all felt smart together.

671   **T**he sixth sitting sheet slitter slit six sheets.

I guess the sheet slitter is back!

672   **T**he tenth table tennis championship challenge.

673   **A**dam's attempted arithmetic answers were always error-riddled.

674 **T**wenty tenors tried tennis.

675 **S**ally spelled six synonyms.

676 **E**leven excited elves eagerly exited.

677 **F**ourteen fickle fairies failed flying.

678 **T**wo tooting toucans clap and tap too.

679 **S**ix hundred and sixty-seven sit-ups sent sick Steve spewing.

680 Seth said six sick spells. The six sick spells Seth said send Sheldon's silliness soaring. Silly Sheldon shouted sixty-six short spells. The sixty-six short spells Sheldon shouted ensured Seth suddenly ceased saying sick spells.

681 Sarah's sixth cycling session surely sucked.

682 The seventh ship sunk the sixth ship.

683 Sammie spent six Saturdays slouching silently on the sofa.

Water Works

Riddles

684 **W**hen will water stop flowing downhill?

When it reaches the bottom.

685 **W**hy does the Statue of Liberty stand in New York Harbor?

Because it can't sit down.

686 **W**hat can be swallowed but can also swallow you?

Water.

687 **W**hat do you get if you jump into the Red Sea?

Wet.

688 **H**ow does a boat show its affection?

By hugging the shore?

689 **W**hat did the Pacific Ocean say to the Atlantic ocean?

Nothing, it just waved.

690 **W**hat's another word for tears?

Glumdrops.

691 **W**hat do you call a snowman with a suntan?

A puddle.

692 **H**ow do you saw the sea in half?

With a sea-saw.

693 **W**hat did one raindrop say to the other?

'Two's company, three's a cloud.'

694 **W**hat do you get if you cross the Atlantic with the Titanic?

About halfway.

695 **W**hy are rivers lazy?

Because they never get off their beds.

696 **W**hy does the ocean roar?

You would too if you had crabs on your bottom.

697 **W**hat goes through water but doesn't get wet?

A ray of light.

698 **W**hat do you call a ship that lies on the bottom of the ocean and shakes?

A nervous wreck.

I just knew we should never have gone out in that storm.
And I'm worried about whether the Earth is flat or not.

699 **W**hat happened when the bell fell into the swimming pool?

It got wringing wet.

700 **W**hat washes up on very small beaches?

Microwaves.

701 **W**hat goes in pink and comes out blue?

A swimmer on a cold day.

702 **W**hat did the waterfall say to the fountain?

'You're just a little squirt.'

703 **W**hat is H2O4?

Drinking.

704 **I** go into water red and come out black what am I?

Hot metal.

705 **W**hat did the ground say to the rain?

'If this keeps up, I'll be mud.'

706 **W**hen a boy falls into the water, what is the first thing he does?

Gets wet.

Tongue Twisters

707 Dripping tap, dip your hat.

708 The big, silver, shiny ship sank.

709 The stricken sinking sailor signalled SOS!

710 Both blue boats brought bait but the boatmen borrowed Braydon's rods.

711 I see the sea is shining and the sun shimmers smartly.

712 **W**et Ron wrestled wringing wet Wally wrongly.

713 **W**rinkly Wally really wasted water.

714 **R**uby ran, rode and read by the wet river bed.

715 **R**uby waded in the raging white water river.

716 **A**lf frowned as he threw the anchor down.

717 **B**o's brother's boat broke.

718 **W**endy renders Ryan's wall when it's wet and rainy.

719 **A** splishy splashy fish was snatched by Mitch.

720 **F**unny Flo floundered while Fay found a floaty.

721 Simon swam and Netty snorkled.

722 Sam swam while Sim swallowed seawater.

723 Splish, splash, swish, squished fish.

724 Blake blew blue bubbles in the bath.

725 Slim Shauna's sure she can swim to shore.

726 Doug dips, slides, slips and dives.

Strange School & Wacky Work

Riddles

727 **W**hy do firemen wear red braces?
To keep their trousers up.

728 **W**ho gets the sack every time he goes to work?
The postman.

729 **W**hat's black when it's clean and white when it's dirty?
A blackboard.

730 **I**f a butcher is two metres tall and has size eleven feet, what does he weigh?
Meat.

731 **W**hy was the archaeologist upset?

Because his job was in ruins!

732 **W**hy do doctors wear masks when operating?

Because if they make a mistake nobody will know who did it.

733 **W**hat did the burglar say to the lady who caught him stealing her silver?

'I'm at your service, Ma'am.'

734 **W**hat did the dentist say to the golfer?

'You've got a hole in one!'

735 **W**hy couldn't the sailors play cards?

The captain was standing on the deck.

736 **W**hy are cooks mean?

Because they beat eggs and whip cream!

737 **W**hat's the difference between a jeweller and a jailer?

A jeweller sells watches and a jailer watches cells.

738 **W**hy can't anyone stay angry with actors?

Because they always make up.

739 **W**hat did the farmer say when he lost his tractor?

'Where's my tractor?'

740 **W**hy did the boy laugh after his operation?

Because the doctor had him in stitches.

741 **W**hy didn't the boy work in the wool factory?

Because he was too young to dye.

742 **W**hy did the farmer plough his field with a steamroller?

He wanted to grow mashed potatoes.

743 **A** teacher, a builder and a hat maker were walking down the street. Who had the biggest hat?

The one with the biggest head.

744 **W**hat is the difference between a bus driver and a cold?

One knows the stops, the other stops the nose.

745 **W**hat time do most people go to the dentist?

Tooth-hurty.

746 **W**hat illness do retired pilots get?

Flu.

747 **H**ow did the dentist become a brain surgeon?

His drill slipped.

748 **H**ow did the comedian pass the time in hospital?

By telling sick jokes.

749 **W**hat type of music do geologists like best?

Rock.

NOW...HOLD STILL WHILE I DRILL...

You'd find dancing to this ROCK MUSIC would be much easier with this quartz. That granite is far too heavy!

750 **H**ow can you tell an undertaker?

By his grave manner.

751 **W**hy do artists make a lot of money?

Because they can draw their own wages.

752 **H**ow do fisherman make nets?

They make lots of holes and tie them together with string.

753 **W**hat did the dentist want?

The tooth, the whole tooth and nothing but the tooth.

754 **W**hat's red, white and brown and travels faster than the speed of sound?

An astronaut's ham and tomato sandwich.

755 **W**hat is a computer's first sign of old age?

It loses its memory.

756 **W**hat do you get when you cross a plumber with a ballerina?

A tap dancer.

757 **W**hy did the computer sneeze?

It had a virus.

758 **W**hat's the difference between a train station and a teacher?

One minds the train, the other trains the mind.

759 **W**hy couldn't the boy go straight home from school?

Because he lived around the corner.

760 **W**hat is the easiest way to get a day off school?

Wait until Saturday.

761 **W**hy was the cross-eyed teacher so frustrated?

Because he couldn't control his pupils.

762 **W**hat trees do fortune tellers look at?

Palms.

763 **I** sometimes build bridges of silver and crowns of gold. Who am I?

A dentist.

764 **W**hat's the difference between a nightwatchman and a butcher?

One stays awake and the other weighs a steak.

Tongue Twisters

765 The assistant principal's announcement signalled silence.

766 Steven suddenly stopped serious science study.

Oh my! I'm giving up science and I'm going to start the biggest stamp collection you've ever seen.

767 Leisel learned lots of lessons at lunchtime.

768 Suspension, expulsion, detention, yard duty.

769 Clara took glasses in cases to class. Clara carelessly cracked glasses in classes. Clara's cracked glasses in cases in classes caused chaos.

770 Aaron, Alex and Arwin arrived at after-school care all alone.

771 Trudy was tardy attending trigonometry; trigonometry truly was a trial for Trudy.

772 Leroy liked learning literature.

773 Peter played politely in the playground at playtime.

774 **H**enrietta's horribly hard history homework was hysterical.

775 **S**irius's sister's slackness ensured slowly slipping science scores.

776 **F**rank finally passed physics after frequently failing.

777 **T**ruant Tracey's truancy tricked teachers.

778 **G**eography is generally geographic.